STRAIGHT TALK

TALK
SEXUALITY EDUCATION FOR PARENTS AND KIDS 4-7

STRAIGHT TALK

SEXUALITY EDUCATION FOR PARENTS AND KIDS 4-7

BY

MARILYN RATNER
AND
SUSAN CHAMLIN

for Planned Parenthood® of Westchester, Inc.

VIKING

VIKING
Viking Penguin Inc., 40 West 23rd Street,
New York, New York 10010, U.S.A.
Penguin Books Ltd, Harmondsworth,
Middlesex, England
Penguin Books Australia Ltd, Ringwood,
Victoria, Australia
Penguin Books Canada Limited, 2801 John Street,
Markham, Ontario, Canada L3R 1B4
Penguin Books (N.Z.) Ltd, 182–190 Wairau Road,
Auckland 10, New Zealand

First published in 1985 by Planned Parenthood® of Westchester, Inc.
This edition with additional illustrations first published in 1987 in
simultaneous hardcover and paperback volumes by Viking Penguin Inc.
Published simultaneously in Canada

Poetry credits:
"Joints" © 1985 by Terry Cooper. Used with permission.
"An Explanation" © 1985 by Bobbi Katz. Used with permission.

LIBRARY OF CONGRESS CATALOGING IN PUBLICATION DATA
Ratner, Marilyn.
Straight talk.
Reprint. Originally published: White Plains, N.Y. :
Planned Parenthood® of Westchester, c 1985.
Bibliography: p.
1. Sex instruction for children.   2. Parent and
child.   I. Chamlin, Susan, 1943–   .   II. Title.
[HQ53.R38   1987]   649'.65   86-15964
ISBN 0-670-81317-6

Printed in the United States of America
Set in ITC Cheltenham

Acknowledgments ──────

This book is the result of parents' demands—for information, advice and support. An enormous amount of energy went into this project and many people contributed suggestions that helped us. With grateful appreciation, the authors acknowledge the efforts of the staff of Planned Parenthood® of Westchester, and the many friends and colleagues who were involved:

Francine Stein, Norma Dreyfus, M.D., Adrienne Rudge, Marian Williams, Elaine Jacobson, Marcia Miller, Stella Kaplan, Irene Kohn, Audrey Drayton, Lynn Keller, Mary Hartshorne, Mary Jane McCann, Elizabeth St. John Villard, Claire Hirschfeld, Sydney Stern, Bobbie Dammann, Terry Cooper, Freddi Friedman, Renata Warshaw, Rev. Richard Martin, Marcia Lawrence, William Lewit, M.D., Marjorie Lewis, Nancy Aranow, Matti Feldman, Harriet Sobol, Mary Stephens, Irma Van Damm, Ph.D., Judith Harary, Morton Berman, M.D., Michael Carrera, Ph.D., Melvin J. Padawer, M.D., Marjorie Schlenoff, Marjorie and Sydney Liebowitz, Marsha Wylie, Susan Tapper, Judith Wilbur, Gloria Lewit, Shelli Pines, Kathleen McIntosh, and Berta Kelly.

We thank our families who are a living part of this book.

Authors' Note _____

We see this workbook as a beginning—a way to establish a more active and open communication between parents and young children. It's important to show a child that you are willing to talk. Children also need to know that you are willing to listen. We hope that parents will continue to look for information and guidance. The bibliography can lead you to additional sources of information and encourage you to pursue the answers to questions that arise in your family.

We hope this workbook has helped parents begin a process that leads to careful, intelligent decisions about sexuality education that reflect their values; these decisions should never make a child feel guilty and ashamed of his sexual self.

We would appreciate hearing from you about how this workbook was used and about issues and questions in your families. Send comments to:

EDUCATION DEPARTMENT
PLANNED PARENTHOOD®
OF WESTCHESTER, INC.
175 Tarrytown Road
White Plains, NY 10607

Contents _____

Foreword _____

As a pediatrician, I am frequently asked questions by parents about how to handle sexual issues with their children. Whether a child is four or fourteen, this is an area where discomfort and confusion abound!

Parents of teenagers express concerns about their child's behavior in this time of "sexual revolution." Initiating discussions around sexuality at an early age lays the groundwork for transmitting parents' feelings and attitudes and paves the way for discussions with children at future dates.

In this book the authors stress communication between parents and their sons and daughters. Although parents and children use similar words their "language" is different. As children grow, their intellectual capacities, just as their bodies, develop and change. When a child asks a question pertaining to sexuality it is important first to understand from the child what he or she really wants to know before answering. Parents often fear that they will say too much. Rest assured, children only "hear" what they are capable of absorbing intellectually.

Many of the principles in this book pertain not only to sexuality but also to general issues of communication between parents and children. It uses charm and imagination to help parents make the very complicated, difficult task of parenting a little bit easier.

Enjoy this book and those very special close times together with your child.

Norma G. Dreyfus, M.D.
Assistant Clinical Professor of Pediatrics
Albert Einstein College of Medicine

A Word on Words _____

Words are important. Much has been written about sex education but this book talks about a broader term: sexuality education. The distinction is significant because in our culture the word "sex" usually refers to sexual intercourse or to gender. Sexuality refers to gender, body image, family roles and the whole experience of being male or female. Sexuality education for a small child includes facts, attitudes, values, feelings and behavior.

It is very hard to write a book on sexuality without being conscious of how we use "he" and "she." Gender is alternated throughout in order to eliminate sexist references and to emphasize that the information is applicable to parents and children of both sexes.

Sexuality Education for Today's Parents ____

- **What should I say when my four-year-old asks, "How do you make a baby?"**

- **Is it normal for a six-year-old to masturbate?**

- **Should my five-year-old be allowed to sleep in my bed?**

- **Why hasn't my preschooler asked about my obvious pregnancy?**

THESE QUESTIONS reflect typical concerns that parents of young children have about sexuality education. Parents today are struggling to do the "right thing." They want to answer questions honestly and respond appropriately to their children's sexual curiosity and behavior. They may worry because a child doesn't ask questions.

While parents want to be able to talk about sexuality, few feel prepared to do so. Some feel they don't know enough. Others are embarrassed. Still others have not clearly defined their own sexual attitudes. The influence of their own upbringing may prevent them from feeling comfortable. Nonetheless, parents want to share *their* values and help their children gain perspective on the sexual messages conveyed by TV, radio, magazines, popular music and peer groups. That's why this book was written.

This book is intended for parents of four- to seven-year-olds. Its purpose is to help parents be more confident and comfortable as the prime sexuality educators of their children. The main focus is communication. A variety of techniques is suggested to help parents begin the process of talking about sexuality issues. You'll find typical questions asked by young children and by parents and suggested answers for both. A unique section is **Kids' Place** — activities especially designed for this age group that will aid in family discussion and communication. You as a parent should adapt the information and advice to your particular needs. After all, you are the best judge of your child and the best teacher. Family situations which include, for example, blended families, single-parent families and adoptive families may require modifying some of the suggestions in this book.

Clearly the task of sexuality education is a difficult, changing and challenging one for parents today. Providing the facts, while an important beginning, is just part of the job. As early-childhood expert Selma Fraiberg points out in *The Magic Years*, "The aim is not only to teach the facts, but to create in the child a group of desirable attitudes toward his own body, the fact of his own sex and his sexual role now and in the future."

This book is a beginning.

———— GOALS ————

You want your young child to ...

- **feel good about being a boy or a girl**

- **know the correct words for body parts and functions**

- **know that sexual feelings are part of being human**

- **know that there is a difference between public and private behavior**

- **come to *you* for correct information**

- **begin to recognize conflicting messages about sexuality on TV and in other media**

- **understand your family's values related to sexuality**

How to Be an "Askable" Parent_____

SEXUALITY EDUCATION would be simple if parents could discuss bodies, gender and "the facts of life" in the same open and honest way they discuss other areas of learning. However, sexuality is a sensitive and delicate area. It includes psychological, social, moral and physical concerns. We all are influenced by our own sexuality education or lack of it. So becoming an "askable" parent may take some doing and undoing.

What is an "askable" parent?
Someone who . . .

- can be approached for information and guidance

- listens to a child and tries to answer questions accurately

- knows what a child is capable of understanding and responding to at different ages and stages of development

- has a sense of humor

- shares feelings that sexuality is a valuable part of being human

- encourages a child to ask for information

- is willing to repeat answers until a child is satisfied with the information

Being askable doesn't necessarily mean waiting to be asked. Perhaps your son has never asked how a pregnancy begins or your daughter seems unaware that she looks different from her brother.

This doesn't mean that the child doesn't want to know. Sometimes a parent needs to initiate discussion either by commenting on something she and her child witness or experience or by asking a question. Suppose that you and your child see a mother breast-feeding. You might say, "That baby is having lunch right from his mother's breast." This matter-of-fact statement shows a child that it's OK to talk about what you saw. Although such discussions may be awkward at first, they can develop into a useful pattern. You want your child to know that any topic is suitable for discussion.

It's important to keep in mind that whether or not sexuality has been discussed, sexual communication takes place between parents and children starting at birth. Much communication is nonverbal. When a parent kisses a baby's belly or strokes her soft skin, he's showing feelings about caressing and about bodies. When a parent pulls a baby's hand away from her genitals, a negative message is given. Facial expressions, gestures and other body language, what is not said—all of these are powerful communicators.

Some parents are afraid of making mistakes by talking too much or too soon about sexuality. Common sense is a good guide. There are many appropriate ways to respond to a child's curiosity. Making a mistake isn't dangerous—one wrong answer does not lead to permanent problems. But a pattern of avoiding questions and making a child feel ashamed of normal, age-appropriate behavior can be damaging. Since sexuality education begins at birth, it's never too early to start.

Dos and Don'ts

THESE ARE some general guidelines for communicating about sexuality with young children.

DO try to relax.

Try to think about sexuality in the same way you think of subjects with which you are comfortable. As a parent you are constantly explaining everything from why it rains to how to use a knife and fork. A child needs help to understand and learn the vocabulary for sexuality issues. You *are* equipped to answer your child's questions. You may need practice. For some parents this may mean saying the parts of the body out loud or reviewing the facts of conception and reproduction.

DO listen to your child's question.

Check with the child to be sure that you understand the question. Asking "What do you think?" will usually get you on the child's wavelength.

DO keep your answer simple.

Although the question might be answered by a volume of the encyclopedia, it doesn't have to be. Give enough information to answer the question *in terms the child can understand.* If you don't know, say, "I don't know, but I'll find out and let you know because I do want to talk."

DO pick the right time.

Just because your son picks the checkout line at the supermarket to ask, "Why is that lady fat?" doesn't mean you have to answer then and there. Tell the child you'll talk about it at home and be sure to follow up later. The answer to "Why is that lady fat?" can be, "That lady is pregnant. She is going to have a baby." If this satisfies the child, there's no need to go any further at the moment. Let your child's interest and questions be your guide.

DO realize the question may not always be what the child really wants to know.

Probe the question to discover what's behind it. You might ask what the child thinks or imagines. For example, suppose that your four-year-old asks, "How does a baby get out?" You might start by asking, "What do you think?" or "Try a guess." If your child doesn't know, you could explain, "Well, we know that a woman has a vagina. The vagina can stretch to be large enough for the baby to come out. Does this explain how a baby gets out?" If the child says no then continue the dialogue. You might say, "What don't you understand?" This might be an ideal time to look at the anatomical drawings on pp. 28-29 together. After this kind of discussion it's a good idea to check what the child "heard."

DO be prepared for repetition.

Even if you tell Joshua at four that a baby starts in a woman's uterus, that doesn't mean that he won't ask at four and a half, five, eight and sixteen.

See repetition as a sign that you're doing a good job. Be glad that the lines of communication are open. You want your child to build on his knowledge as he matures. His curiosity is normal and healthy.

DO educate yourself about child development.

This will make it easier to understand your child's questions and behavior. Knowing what to expect helps you cope with behavior and handle undesirable behavior more effectively. While every child has his own pattern of growth and development, certain behaviors crop up as predictable for certain ages. Most four-year-olds, for example, use bad language. Knowing that this is "a stage" doesn't mean you should ignore it, but it can help you relax about it.

DO try to recognize your child's individual style.

Some children, for example, don't verbalize feelings easily but can express themselves through a puppet show or doll play. You may need to structure a situation where your child can feel free to say what's on her mind. A doll drama about what is going to happen when Mommy goes to the hospital to have a baby may provide the opportunity to answer your child's factual questions and also deal with her feelings.

DO investigate your own feelings about sexuality.

As a parent you have ideas about how to raise and care for your child, how you want her to behave, what you expect her to accomplish. You constantly consider what she eats, how much sleep she gets, her relationships with friends and family. Sometimes a parent has not thought much about sexuality issues before they arise. It's helpful to clarify your values; talk about sexuality with your partner or other adults. Children adopt values from other family members: aunts, uncles, grandparents, siblings. Talking to them, sharing your thoughts and listening to theirs may help you to think more clearly about your attitudes. It's easier to be consistent and available to share your thoughts and feelings when you know how you feel and what you value.

Here's an example: Many parents are not sure whether or not it's appropriate for children to see them undressed. Most parents are not uncomfortable when the child is two or three, but are guarded when the child is four or five or older. If a parent is embarrassed or insecure about being seen undressed but tries not to show it in an effort to be "open," his discomfort will probably still be evident. This can confuse a child. In this situation a parent could simply say, "I feel uncomfortable being naked in front of you." There's no reason a parent should go along with behavior that upsets him. The goal is to convey positive attitudes about bodies and let a child know you feel good about yours.

DO expect to feel uncomfortable.

The important point is to communicate. Many parents have no trouble explaining reproduction but hesitate to mention intercourse or to use the words penis and vagina. Try to recognize areas of discomfort and practice using the correct words. You can always say to a child, "This isn't easy for me to talk about, but I'll try." If discussing a subject is especially difficult, look for another way to present information. Reading a book or watching TV together can trigger communication.

DON'T think you have to know everything.

Children are very inventive, so occasionally a question will catch you off guard. Even if this happens, there is no harm in saying, "I don't know how triplets happen" or "I never thought about how turtles have sex. Let's look it up in a book together."

DON'T always wait for the child to ask.

Children have many reasons for not asking questions. Look for ways to introduce a subject and invite questions. Remember the child's question about the fat lady? A parent can begin discussion with a comment or a question.

DON'T think it's harmful to tell too much too soon.

It's not a catastrophe if you overdo your explanation a bit. The best rule is to give the information the child asked for. If, for example, your son does not understand the complete sperm-and-egg story, remember that conception is a complex subject and it often needs repetition and clarification. Be assured he will ask additional questions at some point giving you another opportunity to explain it.

DON'T make fun of your child's fanciful ideas.

You want your child to know that a baby is not started by swallowing a seed but you can correct her misconception in a positive way. One way is to admire her inventiveness and then explain the true facts.

Being askable takes practice and effort. Try to approach your child's interest in sexuality as you do other areas of his development. If you can be at ease discussing sexuality with your four- to seven-year-old, you will be more successful discussing personal issues in later years. It's important that your child rely on you for information.

Know Your Child _____

THE KINDS OF BEHAVIOR related to sexuality that tend to occur in children four to seven are highlighted on these two pages. Of course, every child develops differently and has his own timetable.

PRESCHOOL Ages four and five

Preschoolers are naturally curious, active explorers, full of questions, ideas and self-initiated activities. They are concrete thinkers and learn best through being able to touch and see. For example, trying to explain thunder may be difficult; a child may cling to the notion that it comes from angels playing drums despite more scientific explanations. After all, she has experience with drums, not with hot and cold air masses.

This is also a time for heightened sex-role awareness, body awareness and playacting.

Behavior related to sexuality

- undressing with another child
- creative play dramatizing "doctor," "hospital" and "birth"
- masturbation
- verbal play about elimination and interest in bathroom activities
- verbalization of romantic attachments toward parent — "I'm going to marry you"
- imitation of adult behavior
- use of obscenity and repetition of "curse" words
- interest in babies, pregnancy and the birth process.

EARLY ELEMENTARY SCHOOL Ages six and seven

In these years children are active, eager to learn, concerned with how things work, what they do and how they are made. Their intellectual processes are concrete. Sixes and sevens exhibit developing awareness of self within a larger social world. They begin to measure themselves against others and absorb impressions from what they see, hear and read.

Behavior related to sexuality

- continuing sex play and masturbation

- increased awareness of differences between the sexes in body structure

- sensitivity to differences between the sexes. Stronger same-sex friendships and increased self-consciousness. Strong interest in male/female roles

- exhibitionism in play situations or in school bathrooms

- exaggerated modesty and desire for privacy

- need for uniformity with peers in dress, speech, etc.

- use of obscenity. Giggling, name-calling or remarks about elimination and bathroom functions

- asking of searching questions about pregnancy, birth and babies. May ask about the father's role in reproduction. Interest in comparing human and animal behavior.

Note that a child's behavior should be seen in the context of his age rather than interpreted using adult standards. Although child and adult behaviors may look similar at times, they must be evaluated differently.

Keep in mind that sex play is just that, actions based on a play situation. Two five-year-olds exploring each other's bodies are not engaged in homosexual behavior. Rather, their natural curiosity is being satisfied through a play situation.

Questions Kids Ask

REMEMBER, there are many "right" ways to answer a question. Your response will depend on the age of the child, what she already knows and what you want her to know. The best rule of thumb is to find out what the child thinks. Take the questions step by step and refer back to the child's actual concerns.

In this book we advise using vocabulary that is accurate and appropriate to young children's understanding. Words like menstruation, fetus and urethra are accurate, yet children may have difficulty using them when they are also learning new concepts. We have selected words which answer the intent of the child's question and which allow easy and relaxed conversation.

Where do babies come from?

This is usually the first question, asked at around three or four. The child often wants to know "Where did *I* come from?"

An easy answer for a younger child is "A baby grows inside a woman in a special place called the uterus." If you do elaborate, correctly identify the *uterus* as the place where a baby develops because many children incorrectly believe it's the stomach. Children also are confused by being told that there's a seed growing inside Mommy because they think of swallowing a fruit pit and conclude that birth is part of the digestive process.

You might also add that there are other words for the developing baby (embryo, fetus) and that it takes nine months until the baby is ready to be born.

Can I have a baby? or Can boys have babies?

Little girls usually want to know that when they are mature they can be mothers. This is a good chance to explain that girls have a special place, called a uterus, where a pregnancy develops and that when they grow up they can have babies.

Boys are often neglected in terms of the male role in reproduction so this is a good time to explain that although a boy cannot give birth to a baby, a baby must have a father. After a baby is born, both mother and father enjoy and care for the child.

There are many variations on this theme. This can be a chance for an adopted child to learn that not all women can have babies and not all men can father a child.

Current news stories may prompt questions related to such subjects as test-tube babies and surrogate mothers. In any special situation, think about *your* child, what she can accept and how much you want her to know at this age. Be accurate.

Why do you have body hair?

Children often notice differences between their bodies and adults'. You can explain that body hair appears, along with other physical changes, when you grow up. Breasts grow, the penis and testicles enlarge, voices deepen. All are part of the physical changes from childhood to adulthood.

Why don't girls have penises?

Sometime in toddlerhood (some experts believe by age two) boys and girls realize that they are anatomically different. You might say to a three- or four-year-old, "I'm glad you noticed that boys and girls have different bodies." Or "Boys are fancy on the outside and girls are fancy on the inside," as TV's Mister Rogers says. The child may be concerned that a girl is missing a penis or that a boy could lose his. Explain that this is not true.

The important information for children is that bodies are different and each body is special in its own way. Use the correct names for body parts. You might want to look at the anatomical drawings on pp. 28-29 as a starting point for discussion.

Why do I have a belly button?

Young children are naturally curious about their bodies, and the navel receives much attention. You may begin by explaining that as a baby develops inside a woman it gets its food and nourishment through a long tube, the umbilical cord. The tube is connected to a special place inside the mother's uterus. "Where your belly button is now is where this tube was attached to you. After you were born it was not needed and it fell off."

Why does my penis get hard?

How detailed an answer you give depends on the child's age. For a younger child, start with, "It's normal for your penis to get hard." Give more information if he shows additional interest. You might say to an older child, "It's normal for your penis to get hard. It happens to men, boys and to boy babies. The penis is very sensitive to touch. Touching or rubbing it feels good and that may make it hard. Sometimes it gets hard for no apparent reason."

When discussing masturbation with an older child it may be appropriate to say that girls and women also masturbate. Explain that girls have a sensitive part in their vulva called the clitoris.

Why is that lady's tummy fat?

"That lady is going to have a baby. She's pregnant." This can be a good opportunity to begin to talk about where and how babies grow and are nourished. You might want to look at a book of photographs to give your child an accurate picture of fetal development. If you are pregnant you can discuss your experience in detail. Of course, much depends on your child's knowledge and interest. Most children adore hearing stories about their own infancy and when their mother was pregnant.

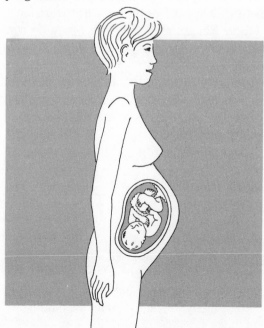

How was I born? or *How does a baby get out?*

The child up to age eight is usually asking for physical details in an effort to understand how things work. Start by finding out what the child knows or imagines. Ask,"What do you think?" Many children are confused about their anatomy. Explain that "A baby comes out of a woman's vagina. The vagina is not the place where urine and bowel movements come out. When a baby is being born the vagina stretches to enable the baby to come out." A child may want to view your vagina. Guide the child to look at herself in the bathtub or in a mirror. Explain that in a little girl, the vagina is a very little opening. As she grows, so will her vagina.

May I see/touch your vagina?/penis?

This question comes from children who are curious about conception and birth or curious in general. If this request makes a parent feel anxious, this might be a good time to mention privacy. You might tell a child that you understand his curiosity, but that for you this part of your body is private. Children may be guided to look at their own bodies. Or you may want to look at the anatomical drawings on pp. 28-29 together. Some children may need the reassurance that as they grow so will their genitals.

How does a baby get in?

This answer will depend on previous conversations with your child, his age and understanding. A three-, four- or five-year-old is often satisfied with "A man and a woman make a baby."

If your child is interested, go further and describe intercourse and conception. You might say "When a man and woman want to have a baby they put their bodies close together. The man's penis gets hard and goes inside the woman's vagina. A fluid called semen with many tiny sperm cells comes from the man's body. One sperm cell joins with an egg in the mother's body and that starts the process that in nine months produces a baby." If you are discussing intercourse with an older child (perhaps eight or older) you want to include the idea that couples have intercourse not only to make a baby but because they find sex with someone they love and care about a pleasurable experience.

Does it hurt to have a baby?

You want to reassure your child that the pain was normal and not overwhelming. You could say,"Yes, it usually does. However, doctors and nurses assist at a birth. Sometimes the baby's father is also there to comfort, support and help the mother. The pain stops when the baby is born. A woman is able to bear the pain because she is so happy to have the baby." Statements such as "You don't know what I went through when you were born" can make a child feel unnecessarily guilty for the pain of her own birth.

What is sex?

Again your answer will depend on the age of the child. A child may want to test your reaction to hearing a "dirty" word. "'Sex' means male and female, the two sexes," is one answer for a four or younger. For an older child you could say, "Most people use the word 'sex' to mean sexual intercourse," and explain it if the child wants to know. You may go on to explain that the word "sex" encompasses feelings, expectations and roles.

Do you and Daddy have sex?
or *Do you and Mommy have sex?*

This question seems to embarrass parents more than any other. Some expect a flood of intimate questions to follow. A simple yes is often sufficient. When you discuss intercourse with your child, point out that grown-ups find sexual intercourse pleasurable and that when he grows up he will feel the same way.

What is a period?
or *What is this (a tampon or sanitary pad) for?*

Explain to a four- or five-year-old that older girls and women have a monthly flow of blood called menstruation or a period. It is a normal, healthy function of a woman's body. (If a child sees you changing a tampon and questions you while you are unprepared to answer, tell her you will answer shortly and then follow through.)

An older child can understand more details. You might say,"Menstruation is the monthly process by which a small amount of blood (four to six tablespoons) leaves the woman's uterus through the vagina. The flow lasts a few days." Explain that a woman uses a sanitary pad or tampon to prevent the flow from staining her clothes. You might also say that menstrual bleeding does not hurt the way a cut finger does when it bleeds. A girl may want to know when she will menstruate. Explain that girls usually have their first period between ten and fourteen but it's also normal to start earlier or later.

It's helpful to connect menstruation and reproduction, especially for an older child. You might explain that each month a small amount of blood and tissue forms a lining in the uterus in preparation for a possible pregnancy. When the woman is not pregnant, menstruation occurs. You can say that after a girl starts to have her period she is physically able to become pregnant.

A discussion of menstruation can include members of both sexes. It's healthy for children to understand and appreciate each other's bodily functions. If you accept and explain menstruation as a natural part of life the child will also.

What is rape?

Children hear about rape on TV, and although it's difficult to explain, a parent should attempt to discuss rape and allay a child's fears. If you've already explained intercourse the next step can be to describe rape as a violent physical attack where a person, usually female, is forced to have intercourse or participate in sexual acts against her will. You could point out that hurting and forcing people to do what they don't want to do is wrong.

If you have not yet discussed intercourse, start by explaining it as a loving, caring, physical and emotional experience. Then rape can be contrasted as a hurtful, unloving act. This is an opportunity to reinforce ideas about loving and caring that normally accompany sexual intimacy.

What is "gay"?

In our society, "gay" may mean various things to a young person. Often the word "gay" or "fag" is used as an insult. First find out what the child thinks. This may lead to a discussion of homosexuality. You can explain homosexuality as a sexual relationship between members of the same sex. Again, how detailed an answer you provide should depend on the child's interest.

What Do I Look Like? ___

YOUNG CHILDREN SHOULD KNOW and use the correct words for body parts and functions. If your son calls his penis "a thing," or your daughter refers to her vagina as "down there," teach the correct terms. Help your child get used to hearing them by using them yourself.

You might make use of these drawings in discussing sexuality with your child.

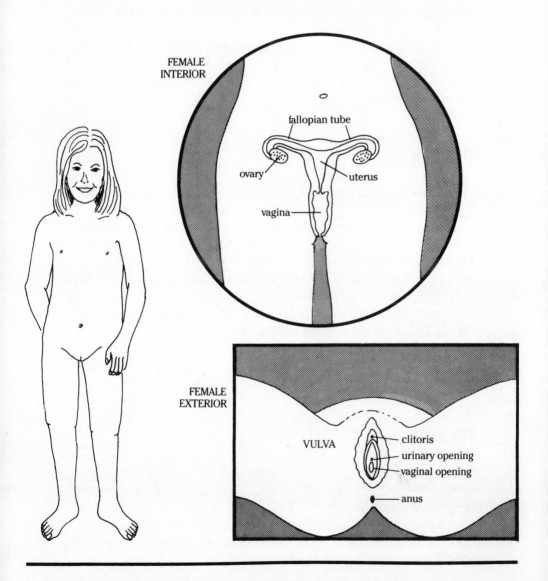

FEMALE
INTERIOR

fallopian tube

ovary

uterus

vagina

FEMALE
EXTERIOR

VULVA

clitoris

urinary opening

vaginal opening

anus

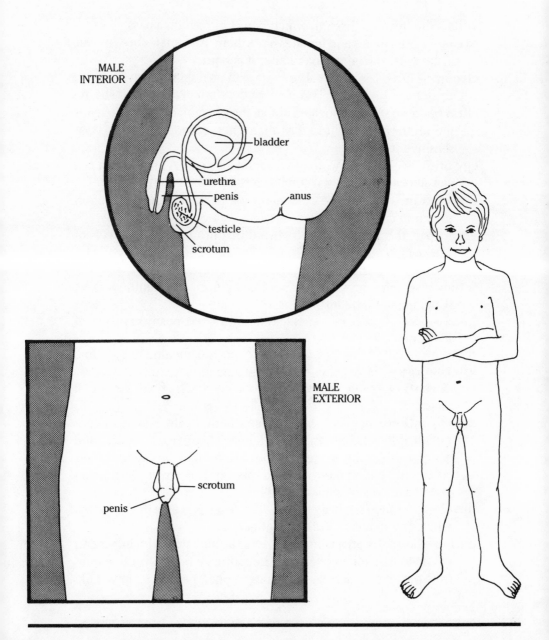

MALE
INTERIOR

bladder

urethra

penis

anus

testicle

scrotum

MALE
EXTERIOR

scrotum

penis

Sexuality Alphabet _____

These are simple explanations of words related to human sexuality. A parent might use these definitions to begin to answer a child's questions. Young children will already be aware of some of the words. It's often necessary to rephrase according to what a child can understand.

anus – the opening through which bowel movements pass.

breasts – both males and females have them. A woman's breasts can make milk to feed her baby after it is born.

circumcision – the removal of loose skin (foreskin) which covers the end of the penis. This is often done when a boy is newborn.

clitoris – a small organ located above the opening of the vagina and the urethra. The clitoris has many nerve endings and is very sensitive to touch.

egg or ovum – this is a woman's reproductive cell. A mature egg cell can start a pregnancy when it is fertilized by a man's sperm.

ejaculation – the release of semen by a penis. During ejaculation urination cannot occur.

embryo – the name given to the third through eighth week of pregnancy.

erection – when the penis gets larger and stiffer.

fetus – the name given to the pregnancy from the eighth week of development until birth.

homosexual – a person who is sexually attracted mostly to people of his or her own sex.

hymen – a fold of skin that partially covers the opening to a vagina.

intercourse – placing the penis in the vagina.

masturbation – rubbing or touching one's own sex organs for sexual pleasure.

menstruation – a stage in a female's body cycle. About once a month, if she's not pregnant, the female's body releases blood and cell tissue from the uterus. It comes out through the vagina. This is commonly called the menstrual period. It normally begins between the ages of ten and fourteen.

navel – also called the belly button. This is the place on the abdomen where the umbilical cord was attached.

nipple – the outlet on a woman's breast through which an infant can get milk. The infant sucks on the mother's breast to draw milk from the nipple. Men also have nipples, but they do not give milk.

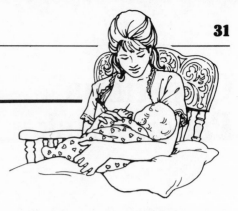

nurse or breast-feed – to feed a baby with milk made in a mother's breasts.

ovaries – female reproductive glands. The two ovaries contain egg cells and also make female hormones that help regulate the menstrual cycle.

penis – a part of the male's body used for urination and sexual intercourse.

scrotum – the pouch of skin behind the penis. Inside are the testes, or testicles.

semen – whitish fluid that comes out of the end of a penis during ejaculation. Semen contains sperm cells and other body fluids.

sperm – these are tiny cells that are contained in semen. A sperm cell can join with an egg cell to start a pregnancy.

sperm

egg

(magnified greatly)

testes or testicles – these are the male reproductive glands. They make sperm and the male hormone.

urethra – the opening through which we urinate. In a male it's at the end of the penis. In a female, it's between the opening of the vagina and the clitoris.

uterus – this is a pear-shaped organ located at the top of the vagina. When a woman is pregnant, the uterus holds the developing fetus.

vagina – an elastic passage in the female that extends from the uterus to an opening in the vulva. The vagina is sometimes called the birth canal.

vulva – the vulva is made up of soft folds of skin called labia or lips. The labia surround the clitoris, urethra and vaginal opening.

Questions
Parents Ask _____

Nudity... masturbation... sex play... homosexuality... child molesting... obscenity. These are the areas of greatest concern to most parents of four- to seven-year-olds. Of course, there's no single right way to handle these delicate issues. You need to recognize your own values and goals and proceed from there. Conveying positive attitudes about healthy sexuality to young children begins the ongoing process that enables them to make thoughtful decisions as teenagers and adults.

● NUDITY AND PRIVACY

Is parental nudity bad for youngsters?

The intimacy of family life naturally includes nudity, and many parents feel perfectly comfortable undressing in front of children and bathing with them. This is fine *if you are comfortable*. Don't put yourself in an uncomfortable situation just to be "modern."

It's also important to observe what your child is comfortable with. Nudity can be troublesome for children at certain ages. It depends on the child. Observe your child. Does he wait outside your room to watch you dressing? Is he overly eager to touch you? For some children, family nudity is overstimulating. If you suspect that nudity is causing discomfort, don't expose the child to it.

Is nudity among children healthy?

Your children have probably had opportunities to see other children undressed. Most nursery schools have coed bathrooms. This is perfectly normal and a good opportunity for young children to learn and accept physical differences. Sixes and sevens often become spontaneously modest, and parents should respect their children's privacy.

When is privacy necessary?

Many children in this age group want to touch and explore parents' bodies. Some parents are able to comply; others are troubled by this. Am I too permissive if I allow it? Am I too restrictive if I say no? Again, a parent must ask himself, "Am I comfortable?" If a parent is embarrassed he can say, "You are curious about my body. I will tell you how grown-ups are made." This offers the child a way to channel his curiosity into a discussion.

Parents have a right to close the bathroom or bedroom door and ask a child to knock. A child has the same right, and by six or seven most children seem to want some privacy in the bathroom or when dressing. If a child continually barges in on you, explain that grown-ups like privacy just as children do. "Let's talk about some things people like to do in private." Again, this type of conversation accomplishes two things: curiosity is channeled into acceptable behavior and a child is encouraged to talk about her feelings.

What if a child walks in on adults making love?

No one welcomes this invasion of privacy. Initially you may panic, but all is not lost. If you calmly tell a child that you are doing something private and guide him out of the room, he will surely get the message. Sometime later you might give the child a chance to discuss what happened. Some children may conclude that intercourse involves being hurt or angry, and you want to dispel this impression.

Is it wrong for a child to sleep in a parent's bed?

Many experts caution against this as being sexually stimulating and confusing if it becomes a common practice. In addition, if a child routinely sleeps in a parent's bed this diminishes the child's ability to be a separate, independent person. And it denies parents the privacy they deserve. However, there is nothing wrong with the snuggling that parents and children enjoy when a child has a nightmare or is ill or just needs comforting.

How do I deal with my older child's request to breast-feed when I am breast-feeding the baby?

When an older child sees her newborn sibling breast-feeding, she often wants to try it. Attempt to discover what prompts this request. The older child may be expressing a need for extra cuddling and be jealous of the physical closeness between mother and baby. Spending additional time alone with the older child may be helpful. Or the child may want to taste the milk. You could express some milk and put it on your finger for the child to taste. If you are comfortable with allowing her to satisfy her curiosity by breast-feeding, that's OK too.

● SEX PLAY

What should I do when I find my child playing "doctor" or "hospital"?

Somewhere around age four most children play these games. It's helpful to remember that they engage in sex play because they are curious. Even so, parents tend to see the implications of adult sexuality in the child's behavior. This is rarely the case. A parent who wants to interrupt the game might say, "I know you are curious about each other's bodies. Let's talk about what you want to know."

There are several factors to watch for in terms of your child's sex play. One is injury. Many children attempt to take each other's rectal temperature with pencils, sticks or thermometers. Naturally, in this case you need to intervene.

Another issue is your child's self-esteem. Some children are victims of other children's excessive curiosity. If so, you need to step in and help. You might say something like, "You can tell someone no if you don't want him to touch or kiss you. Your body is yours to protect and care for." Children should know that they are special and important and in charge of their own bodies.

It's important to look at the ages of the children in relation to their behavior. It's perfectly normal for children of about the same age to engage in sex play with members of the same or opposite sex. There is cause for concern, however, if one of the children is several years older. Furthermore, if sex play is the child's main activity or mode of play, you might seek professional advice.

● MASTURBATION

Is masturbation normal?

Many parents feel anxious about masturbation and troubled about how to handle it. Most children fondle their genitals. It's perfectly normal and not harmful. It's also normal not to masturbate. As with sex play, there's no "right" way for a parent to respond to masturbation; but a child should not be made to feel guilty about her interest in her body. It's perfectly OK, however, for a parent to help an older child, say four and older, find a private place for this activity. Many four-year-olds can understand the difference between public and private behavior and are able to control their impulses. You might say to a child, "I understand that touching your penis feels good. It is OK in the privacy of your room but it is not OK at the dinner table." This sets limits for the child.

If a child masturbates excessively and does not seem happy in school, or in other areas of his life, this may be a signal that something is wrong. It could be quite simple: For example, a girl might have a vaginal infection requiring medical attention. Parents need to look at the child's overall behavior to determine if professional help is necessary.

● SEX ROLES

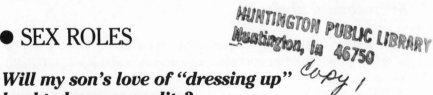

Will my son's love of "dressing up" lead to homosexuality?

No. Many parents discourage boys from playing "dress-up" and "house," but at certain ages, certainly preschool, it's appropriate. Preschoolers actively assume many different roles. Girls try to stand up when they urinate. Boys pretend to breast-feed babies. Both sexes experiment with makeup. Older children like dramatic role-play and often want to dress up for a show. In most cases pretend games are one more way that children imitate and learn about the adult world.

● CHILD MOLESTING

When and how should I warn my child about child molesting?

It's important for children to know at an early age, especially when they walk to school or wait for a bus alone, that *not all adults can be trusted*. A good time to talk is *before* the child goes out without you. Emphasize to the child that he has control over his body and it's OK to say no to an adult. You could say, "Do not allow anyone to touch you or do anything to your body that *you* don't think feels right." While many parents warn their children about strangers, it is unfortunate but true that when children are abused it is most often by someone they know.

A child should be told that if he feels threatened he should look for help. Tell him the names of some adults he can turn to if you are not there. Of course, it's impossible to cover every situation. Your aim is to reassure your child, not to frighten her, so have this discussion in a relaxed way at an appropriate time.

Stress that if anything does happen, the child should tell you and you will not be angry. Your child should understand the difference between private and secret. Explain that if someone does something to her body and wants her to keep it a secret, this could be because it was wrong. Make sure the child understands that you want her to tell you if she is abused in any way.

How can I teach my children to protect themselves from sexual abuse?

Children who feel good about themselves, who have been encouraged to express their feelings and who have accurate and age-appropriate information about sexuality are less likely to become victims of an abuser. Building on these concepts, parents can also create additional learning opportunities for their children by practicing how to judge real or imaginary situations.

You could draw on reports from the media and ask your children what they would say or do in a specific situation, or how they think another child might handle a similar problem. You may also offer your children some general guidelines for real situations in their lives: for example, who is permitted to pick them up at school; the best way for you and your family to answer the telephone; the safest route to walk to school. Experts advise that it is perfectly all right to teach your children to say no to anyone who tries to touch, kiss, or play a secret game that makes them feel uncomfortable. It's essential that your children know they can always tell you about such an occurrence.

● OBSCENITY

How should I react to "dirty words"?

Kids like to repeat words even when they don't know their meanings. "Shit," "fuck," "screw" and "fag" are popular with this age group. Usually a child is testing to see how a parent will react. There's no reason to be shocked and upset about obscenity, but a parent certainly has the right to discourage it.

Check the child's knowledge. You might say, "That's interesting. What does it mean?" Then help her learn what the word means and tell her when she may and may not use it. Teach your child some acceptable words to use to express anger and frustration. It's also helpful to explain that these words may bother others.

Bibliography ————

TO FURTHER INVESTIGATE the sexuality issues raised in this workbook, refer to these useful, recommended books. This list is by no means intended to be complete. It's a good idea to preview books for young children for level of difficulty, and to match the needs and interests of your child.

Books for Parents

Arnstein, Helene. *What to Tell Your Child.* New York: Condor Publishing Co., 1978.

Calderone, Mary, and Johnson, Eric W. *The Family Book About Sexuality.* New York: Harper and Row, 1981.

Carrera, Michael. *Sex: The Fact, the Acts & Your Feelings.* New York: Crown Publishing, 1981.

Child Study Association of America. *What to Tell Your Child About Sex.* New York: Pocket Books, 1974.

Dodson, Fitzhugh. *How to Parent.* New York: New American Library, 1973.

Fraiberg, Selma. *The Magic Years.* New York: Charles Scribner's Sons, 1959.

Gordon, Thomas, and Wyden, Peter. *Parent Effectiveness Training.* New York: New American Library, 1975.

Ilg, Frances L., M.D., and Ames, Louise Bates. *Child Behavior from Birth to Ten.* New York: Harper and Row, 1955.

Planned Parenthood® Federation of America. *How to Talk with Your Child About Sexuality.* New York: Doubleday and Co., 1986.

Selzer, Joae. *When Children Ask About Sex: A Guide for Parents.* Boston: Beacon Press, 1975.

Books to Share—Factual Books About Sex/Anatomy

deSchweinitz, Karl. *Growing Up. How We Become Alive, Are Born and Grow.* New York: Collier Books, 1974.

Gordon, Sol, and Cohen, Judith. *Did the Sun Shine Before You Were Born? A Sex Education Primer.* Fayetteville, New York: Okpaka Communications, 1974.

Rayner, Claire. *The Body Book.* New York: Barron's Educational Series, 1980.

Books to Share—About Roles

Thomas, Marlo, et al. *Free to Be... You and Me.* New York: McGraw-Hill, 1974. (Also available as a recording.)

Waxman, Stephanie. *What Is a Girl? What Is a Boy?* Culver City, CA: Peace Press, 1976.

Books to Share—About Babies/Siblings

Anacona, George. *It's a Baby!* New York: E. P. Dutton, 1979.

Andry, Andrew C., and Schepp, Steven. *How Babies Are Made.* New York: Time-Life Books, 1968.

Gruenberg, Sidonie M. *The Wonderful Story of How You Were Born.* New York: Doubleday, 1973.

Holland, Vicki. *We Are Having a Baby.* New York: Charles Scribner's Sons, 1972.

Levine, Milton I., and Seligmann, Jean H. *A Baby Is Born.* New York: Western Publishing Co., 1978.

Mayle, Peter. *Where Did I Come From?.* Secaucus, NJ: Lyle Stuart, 1973.

Nilsson, Lennart. *A Child Is Born.* New York: Delacorte Press, 1977.

_____. *How Was I Born? A Photographic Story of Reproduction and Birth for Children.* New York: Delacorte Press, 1977.

Stein, Sara Bonnet. *That New Baby.* New York: Walker and Co., 1974.

Children's Books About Babies/Siblings

Alexander, Martha. *Nobody Asked Me If I Wanted a Baby Sister.* New York: Dial Press, 1971.

Berenstain, Stanley and Jan. *The Berenstain Bears' New Baby.* New York: Random House, 1974.

Dragonwagon, Crescent. *Wind Rose.* New York: Harper and Row, 1976.

Hazen, Barbara S. *Why Couldn't I Be an Only Kid Like You, Wigger?* New York: Atheneum, 1975.

Hoban, Russell and Lillian. *A Baby Sister for Francis.* New York: Harper and Row, 1976.

Hurd, Edith Thatcher. *The Mother Beaver.* Boston: Little Brown, 1971.

Wolde, Gunilla. *Betsy's Baby Brother.* New York: Random House, 1982.

Kids' Place

THESE ACTIVITIES are designed to encourage communication between you and your child about bodies, family life, sex roles and feelings. They reinforce the concepts of this workbook: that children learn to know, understand and feel good about their bodies and that families should have open communication about sex and sexuality. Since you know your child best, choose the activities that suit your needs and vary them for your situation.

The activities are divided into those suitable for fours and fives and those suitable for sixes and sevens. The younger group will need your instruction and close supervision. Older children should be able to do many of the projects fairly independently but may need your help to explain the project and get it started. The activities are deliberately open-ended, designed to stimulate discussion, not to lead to a right answer. We have listed a goal for each activity to help focus your thoughts and explain what your child may gain from the activity.

Pull out the following eight-page section and fasten or place in a binder. ▶

Kids' Place

Boy or Girl?

Goal: *to recognize male-female differences in nature.*

How can you tell a boy from a girl? Many living things make this easy—they look different. Look at the drawings. Which are the males? Which are females? Draw your own male and female living things.

1

Baby Animals

Goal: *to learn about animal reproduction.*

Visit a zoo or pet shop to see baby animals. Find out how chickens reproduce. What about dogs and cats? Go to the library and look at books about baby animals.

Feeling Faces

Goal: *to recognize the range of emotions.*

Make faces in the mirror—a happy face, sad face, baby face, monster face, silly face. Ask your child to pick a feeling face and make up a story about it. Discuss the ways in which boys and girls show their feelings.

Face Hunt

Goal: *to identify feelings and learn vocabulary to explain them.*

On a shopping trip pay attention to faces. Point out someone who looks happy, worried, excited, angry. Help your child find a word or phrase to describe how the person looks. Ask him to imagine why a person might feel that way.

Role-Playing Kits

Goal: *to try out stereotypical sex roles through dramatization.*

An activity for a child to do with friends or siblings. You supply the props, the kids do the pretending. Organize props for each kit in a paper bag. Each child or group chooses a kit and makes up a skit using the props.

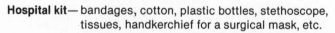
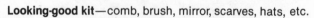

Office kit—pencils, paper, play telephone, empty cartons for pretend office equipment.

Hospital kit—bandages, cotton, plastic bottles, stethoscope, tissues, handkerchief for a surgical mask, etc.

Looking-good kit—comb, brush, mirror, scarves, hats, etc.

Restaurant kit—plates, silverware, apron, napkins, glasses, pretend menus, etc.

School kit—pencils, paper, books, crayons, blocks.

2-D Bodies

Goal: *to identify body parts.*

Make a life-size poster of your child's body. Lay a large piece of paper on the floor and have your child lie down on it. Trace the body outline. Cut out the body. Together decorate the cutout with hair, eyes, nails, etc. You might make two bodies—one clothed, one undressed. For the undressed body include the navel, breasts, penis or vagina, knees, etc. Ask the child to compare how he or she looks with how friends and other family members look.

Family-Tree Poster

Goal: *to understand the physical similarities and differences among people.*

Collect photos of family members and organize them on a large sheet of construction paper into the design of a family tree. (If photos are not available, draw the relatives.) This is one way for a child to begin to recognize similarities and differences in physical appearance. Whom does she look like? Who has curly hair? Blue eyes? etc.

Making a family-tree poster is a good opportunity to talk about different kinds of families. Who makes up his family? Who are the key people in his life? Who are the members of the families of people he knows?

Rebus

Goal: *to have fun with body vocabulary.*

A rebus is a picture puzzle. Help your child solve this one. Then make up your own together.

Boys look like boys, girls look like girls. But what does everyone have?

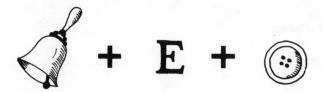

Answer: A belly button.

Who Does the Laundry?

Goal: *to identify the different jobs of family members and eliminate stereotypes.*

Many chores that used to be done mainly by mothers are now being done by fathers too. Who does your family's jobs? Which chores do you do? Write the name of the person or persons in your family who do each chore. Compare your list with a friend's list.

Chores	**Who does it?**
Washing clothes	_____
Ironing	_____
Fixing your bike	_____
Washing dishes	_____
Setting the table	_____
Putting out the garbage	_____
Making the beds	_____
Cooking dinner	_____
Cleaning up after a pet	_____
Bringing in the mail	_____
Making breakfast	_____
Giving you a bath	_____
Buying groceries	_____
Raking leaves	_____
Washing the car	_____
Fixing broken toys	_____

Interest Inventory

Goal: *to help eliminate stereotypes and recognize similarities and differences between boys and girls.*

What do you like to do? Which activities do you think are for boys only? Which are for girls only? Put a check in the boy or girl column. Check both columns if it's something boys *and* girls like to do. Discuss your answers with a parent.

Interest	Boys	Girls
Roller skate	_____	_____
Play baseball	_____	_____
Draw pictures	_____	_____
Build a castle	_____	_____
Bake cookies	_____	_____
Write in a diary	_____	_____
Play a musical instrument	_____	_____
Braid hair	_____	_____
Read a book	_____	_____
Ride a bike	_____	_____
Watch TV	_____	_____
Your favorites		
_____	_____	_____
_____	_____	_____

Be a Reporter

Goal: to learn about pregnancy.

Interview a pregnant friend or relative. Find out the facts. Find out her feelings. You might want to tape-record the interview for the future. Here are some questions to get you started. Add your own questions to this list.

When will the baby be born?
What sex child are you hoping for?
How does it feel to be pregnant?
How do you think your life will be different
    after the baby is born?
In what ways do you think life will be the same?
Why did you decide to have a baby?

_____

_____

_____

Body Poems

Goal: to have fun with body language.

Here are two simple "body poems." Make up your own poem about your body.

An Explanation

In the middle of their tummies
        everybody's got
an innie or an outie
        belly-button knot.
It doesn't help kids
        throw a ball
        smile a smile
        or wink.
The reason they have them
        is to show their friends,
I think!

Bobbi Katz

Joints

Elbows
Ankles
Wrists
Knees
Dependable bendables.

Terry Cooper

Story Timeline

Goal: *to recognize and appreciate physical growth and change.*

What were you like as a baby?
When did you learn to ride a bike?
How did you celebrate your birthday each year?
Ask a parent, grandparent or close friend to tell
you a story about you growing up. Then it's
your turn to tell a story. Look through the
family photo album. Notice the ways in which
you've changed. Tell a story about the baby
that grew to be you.

Friendship Checklist

Goal: *to identify values.*

Brave, lovable, tough. . . what qualities do you look for in a friend?
Check the words that describe a good friend now. Write two checks if you
think you'd like that quality in a husband or wife later on. Discuss your
choices with a parent. Now ask your parents to name the qualities they
look for in a friend or partner.

funny _____

smart _____

strong _____

agreeable _____

quiet _____

caring _____

tough _____

affectionate _____

fun-loving_____

trustworthy _____

bossy _____

talkative _____

shy _____

honest _____

fair_____

other _____

Fabulous Facts

Goal: to initiate discussion about babies and bodies.

Survey your family and friends. You're the expert. You ask the questions.

Q Who has more bones, an adult or a baby?

A A baby has over 300; an adult has 206.

Q True or false, a woman is born with all the eggs she will ever have.

A. True.

Q What is the largest organ in the human body?

A Skin.

Q Which takes more muscles, to smile or to frown?

A To frown (43 muscles). To smile (17 muscles).

Q True or false, more girl babies are born than boy babies?

A False—for every 100 girl babies there are 104 boys.

Q True or false, most boys start growing moustaches at age nine.

A False. Most boys start at puberty, about age twelve.

Q True or false, baby girls smile more than baby boys.

A True.

Q What is the largest muscle in your body?

A Buttock.

? ? ? ? ? ? ? ? ? ? ? ?

What if . . .

Goal: to act out "tough" situations and express feelings through role-play.

Role-play some of these situations with a friend or sibling. Let your own ideas and feelings be aired. Next make up your own *What if...* stories.

- *What if...* your older sister keeps calling you a crybaby. *Get her to stop it.*

- *What if...* you and your brother like to play "doctor" only you both always want to be the doctor. *Convince him that he should be the patient this time.*

- *What if...* your camp group is told to change into swimsuits in a room shared by boys and girls. *Explain to the counselor how you feel about this.*

- *What if...* you want to sleep naked but your mother insists that you wear pajamas. *Discuss this dilemma with her.*

- *What if...* your sister comes into the bathroom while you are going to the toilet and refuses to leave. *Explain your need for privacy.*